REVELATION

BY
BIOR AGUER

CONTENTS

I. PART OF THE PLAN

II. FORMATION

III. PROCLAIMED BY JOHN GARANG

Illustrators: Bior Bior & Piath Thuc Photographer: Owen Haig

 ISBN:9780646878522

PART I.

PART OF THE PLAN

"Living a heroic life is knowing your mortality, how will you run the leg of life? Unveiling the mask?"

Noun (Ruach)

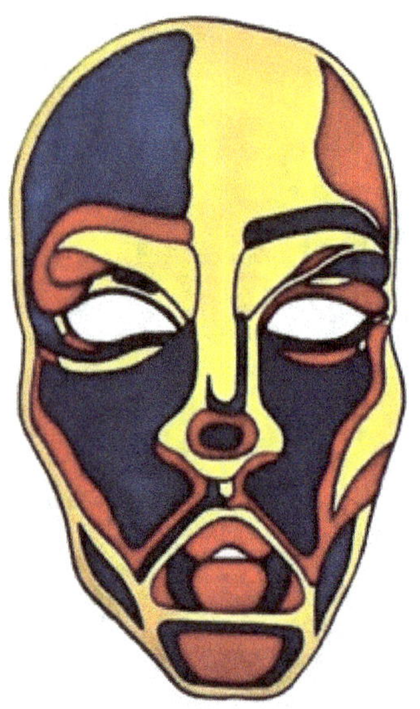

Variations of a similar term, "spirit of God", also appear in various places in the Hebrew Bible. The Hebrew noun ruacḥ (can refer to "breath", "wind", or some (רוח invisible moving force ("spirit").

I am like the Sun rising adjacent to a
local coastline, a beacon

of new age, streaming in new light
inhaling in a new horizon.

A 'ruach' breathing in new light. I plant
myself current to the days as cosmic rays
thus the path swallowed by darkness.

I have never un-pack human interactions, quiet by nature. I sense demise in your pupil,
frequently on my venture
outside myself, I remain

observant.

I may not hold physical wealth although in
my possession weald spiritual wealth it
channels my every movement and beliefs.

My virgin divine
consciousness,
shouts! 5
to me periodically.
It is well.

To be

Me with no

fear.' An

understanding

of oneness,

a connection to all beings, a unity in the vast expanse of the universe. Each breath I take resonates with the heartbeat of Mother Earth, grounding me in the present moment. As I navigate this world with a gentle spirit and open mind, I find solace in the simplicity of existence.

The whispers of the wind guide my steps, leading me towards a deeper understanding of my purpose. Through moments of stillness and reflection, I uncover the beauty of vulnerability and the strength in embracing my true self. In the dance of life, I move with grace and intention, honoring the interconnectedness of all living things.

With each passing day, I embrace the journey of self-discovery with courage and compassion. I am a vessel of light, a beacon of love and acceptance in a world often shrouded in darkness. And as I continue to walk this path of enlightenment, I find peace in knowing that I am exactly where I need to be - in harmony with the universe, in harmony with myself.

Oddly on reason,

I may be smeared oddly,

in symmetry with, trees,

the birds,

my Neighbours catch
me offbeat.

Good news I hoof to a tune

like no other.

I am no ordinary man.

Do these confidences frighten you,
let's not be like talking

marts,

rather look deep rather with glaring
eyes of critique.

Undress hostility as it can seep past skin into your blood vessels.
Infectious towards man-kind as history will reflects. I am lightweight in every present moment so are you and I.
Did you get the message 'you are it.'

I identify as an entity of free will,
a descent of a laborious

tribe carrying on like sound and matter to
great frequency.

Wonders of life, I am close to the gates of my afterlife.

I am Christ Conscious with a message for you.

This building block is simple whether you like me or not, let's not pretend like the others, do you get this picture I am painting?

I am unveiling your contempt for ignorance.

My arrow ticks and clicks on different paths, an age of self-worth.
Flowing from my thoughts and feelings,
shall I never be

measured with notes and coins in my
wallet.

Rather
a smiley face on, these ocean eyes,

I noticed a tale of a rich man of
heart and soul.

Dictated by thoughts and emotions we could never free ourselves from ourselves.

Have we taken the plunge?

Towards you?

Unleashing out for aid?

Reflective of the heart given
from the twilight into a wish.

A

promise.

due north

a student of thy fate.

The galaxy will never give

up, until you subsist your

calling, out towards the

light.

This onus will always remain on

you. Vulnerability is a muscle.

I was not taught in school.

I am training the senses for a war within me.

My consciousness is on trail,

a voice in time,

if you read between these lines.

I am hoping, you listen,

or feel

this message.

I am accountable with

yin and yang around me.

Human intellect,

dwells in the realm of now.

Occasionally I am asked for my
opinion,

I have scanned my vessel internally
and externally.

You might see me as peculiar.

Playing the tough guy on your journey
outside yourself

creates a mask.

Construction on the outside,

to the
inside of
your mind.

Increasi
ng like
water

or the
leaves on
the oak
tree,
as we grow
out of our
world.

How do you
know right
from wrong?

In a spiritual concern
given like our ten
commandments?

If you were to reach peace?
Would you be satisfied?
If you have questioned
your purpose?
Excavate within,

to speak your prophetic declaration, no one else will.

A course of desired… love is rocky,
deceitful,
Misleading,

It's trying to love.

A heart with a connection,

with pain displays a nova of understanding,
ancient as time.
Memories the flow,

in symmetry with purposeful work.

In a flow state,

cells in my bloodstream dance,

tunes of a man on duty,

a living spirit... not talking to you as a command but rather free-spirited.
A love notes,

within vibrating a turn
between you and I
unattached from this physical realm.

Laughter will never be commanded but we seek.

Visions,

of a broken man,

crawling to redemption,

lost in time separated from the pack, observe

me if you must.

Dream…

for love.

Devotion.

Oneness with myself,

love others.

The angels fly
because they take
themselves lightly,

Who knew the
dance of life
began with me?

Salvation

is ever-evolving.

The competition begins in the mind;
most folktales will contest
with countless heroes before me. Watch

me rise!

The violin,

strings
out
a sound.

so pure

my heartbeat… pours,
one sound.
I devote
my tears,
to the next…

generation.

Visions
of a broken
man

crawling to redemption,

lost in time separated from the pack,
follow me if you must.

A warrior
of conclusions. Iam
delegating

my fortune to a living organism, so I let go,
and trust in my given abilities.

In this extreme moment of redemptive
times, I have selected to fall within,
who I am,

a tear and a smile in time.

One with character,

you can describe;

My personality…peaceful.

My heart listens,

because God deals
with reason and passion.
She brought to me

a fullness the world could not offer
man.
It was,

half a hope to find myself.

She
held

the key to,
my other half.
For
half, a
life,

is not yet lived, and may never be.

Postponed in time.

She

told me about love and I listened.

The most lavish virtue attained.

A chance

with your other half, a fractured heart,

her tendered

hand

would,

stir,

it in place.

I am!

peaking

for

my northern star?

from an unknown source.

It speaks to,

me.

Daily,

beyond,

a route,
less travelled searched by many.
A valley

feted with intention, approaches with ease.

I

have a message
as ancient as the Saharan sands.
King Soloman,
presences echo the skies
I respond,

to my father with tenacity.

Deliverance

is served

within the deep
injuries of,
your soul.

An ego fails,

surrendering

to your divine,

will.

An out-of-body experience.

This dark body, and soul

articulates
higher couscous.
If you,
ask me
who I am.

I am one,
with the lord,
who is one with me.

Sing a tune,

with me,
a melody of solitude,
a story of conquest of thy

self.

If uncertainty
was a word,
I would be the mascot,

Someone with masks in their

arsenal,

I have no identity shaping

within me anymore.

Little,

did I know

This was part of the plan.

Flourish,

within the mask.

I was destined to be,

to walk life's journey,

I have never feared fate.

Shaping the legs of
my day,

like the madman
Iam.

Many times

you will never attend to your,
heartbeat
play a symphony to you.

Small

sparks will

flare,
until you investigate
and study your vessel,

your heart wants you to play your music. Are you

hearing me?

My peers, ask me
occasionally.

'How do I get
into the driver's
seat of my life?

The air

is in tune with me; It fuels

me like menthol.

Follow along with my spirit. Iam

freer than you think,

Yes,
I
can.

drunk with life.

I perspire
past the limitations of
man.

Peace

costs,

me

relaying the steps,

I take it.

I dare

not miss a step

    from what I someday,

might earn.

There is always a plan,

answer your demons,

with

I
wil
l.

In the present time,

it may be the beam, from the mind

we tend to ignore,

so I listen.

If I self-indulge

and close my mind?

Clothed

with self-inflicted wounds

I became mates, with my mind.

I am

South Sudanese,

  the long-written song of

champions
of the day,

victorious
with spirit.

We

conquer

misfortune shaped as a fist

we

are front line

of a fight

for

humility and identity.

I am

South Sudanese and

I am
Kush.
I am

a legacy, rewritten,

a million times.

A

transformer of fate. Iam

a

reflection

of greatness

with a page,

yet
turned.

The newspaper seeks an image of
me

as a criminal?

A continuation,

of a paradox

of separation,

of you and me.

When is the right time?

Where is my frame?

Where is my tribe?

I

had

to wander

in the darkness
alone,
and became dark.

Enjoy

the journey,

and own
your happiness.
Take it,
away
from those
who demand it.
A transformer,

when it comes to fate,

wait until you get,
to know me.
I am a reflection of greatness with a page yet turned.

PART II.

FORMATION

"You go through life,
and survive it as a
revelation for

connecting,

giving and
influencing."

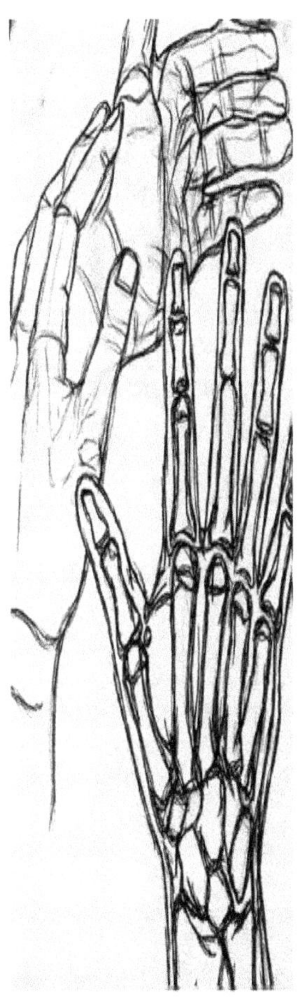

Artists can create a mask,
our surroundings,
lock us in a prison of our
demise
searching for identity.
At best
I love the best-seeking none in
return, a love capsule
in palm
and I offered it

freely.

Still penciling in
my ambitions,

in and out
of consciences
living for the next
moment, we forget
the moment
I was grounded
in time playing the rate race
of life looking for clarity.
living now as living for later
is not in alignment
with the call;
it's all in the steps rather than the destination.

I once did not believe,

I once did not see,

and

I once could not be a vocalist.

For my heart to stand up for me.

I once was overlooked

then I saw,

I saw the bowl

of life

could be tamed

at this moment

I chose to live

outside my mind.

I choose to believe.

Iam

formless in pain

and gathered from the sand

beaming strength

from my notepad

If I?

became

your soul's microphone,

sing
wit
h
me.

Let us rip the fabric of shame...

and destitute,

a shadow

expired.

We have chosen to turn

away from sorrow

into a message.

an instruction from the divine.

Do you believe it?

Do you believe in fairy tales?

Do you believe in
a creator?

Do you believe in yourself?

In your gifts and abilities?

Have you given yourself a chance to

dance?

A chance to play, a chance to say yes?

Then no

a chance to dance,

a chance to believe,

a chance to remember

your worth to stand tall?

To remember

who you are and what you are.

If

you

have forgotten your strength?

Iam

the symbol

of an apostle

returning

from the desert

wiser and driven

in a dream larger

than my understanding. I say here I am

ready to serve.

Mum, Grandma

and my
siblings prayed
for me
before I knew prayer, they gave,

before they had... breath

to a rib
they did not know.

Forget
what you know,
what you see,
never back, remember
these strides as
you try unpack
me, find me
at your
true self
Where
we may
have a conversation about
you and me.

I chose
to believe
before I
or
those around me believed.

Visions
of a broken man
crawling
to redemption
lost in time
separated
from the pack… Follow me…
if you must.

A warrior

of decisions

I am

delegating

my destiny

to a living organism so I let go

and

trust

in my given abilities,

giving myself to others in
an act of principle.

In this revolutionary,

moments of redemptive times,

I have chosen to fall

within

who

I am

a

tear

and

a smile in time.

One

with nature you can describe my

nature as peaceful.

My heart listens

because

God deals with

reason and passion.

She brought to me

a wholeness

the world could not offer

man.

Let's talk

about

the awakening

of a generation

from South Sudan who

had shaken hands

with misfortune

with their elderly

on the front

lines

as they gasped for air.

Speak

about

spiritual awakening

speaks

about

the seeds of

South Sudan

their dreams

were

all buried

then the grave overflowed and

they took

on the world

and made it theirs,

for the taking.

I find

happiness

when
I am free-thinking.
Free-spirited
in sync with the wind we breathe.

Persecuted by my hard times,
I seek a light brighter in the distance
a path less travelled
uncommon to many.
Revelation is something that comes after pain.

We all have substance within our tone
which has been asleep
for quite some time. Let's switch places,
for a minute.

Can you
just take a minute
to acknowledge
this revelation within?

PART III.

PROCLAIMED

BY

JOHN GARANG

"*The world may break you good or bad, it is about how you own it. The going keeps going in our strange view of the world; it is the hallelujah of our participation with life's dance. For those who have come before me and with*

the cost and path they have taken I have laid my heart on the line and taken the responsibility to pass the baton.

It's worth it."

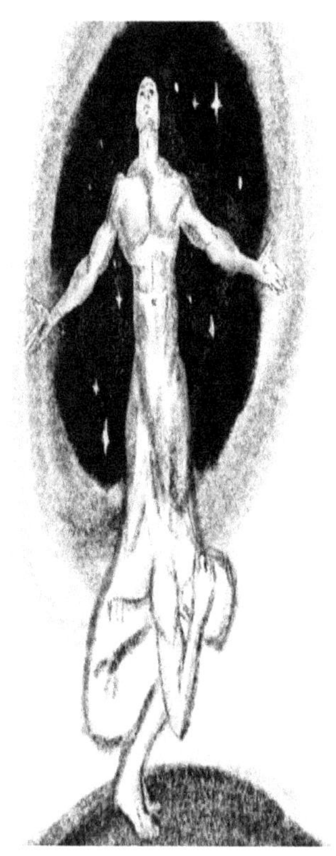

Colonel John Garang de Mabior opened a flame for generations to come with the unsung blissful tale of John Garang.

a voice in the darkness we seek to wake still from. a sleeping hollow of a moment's bliss.

A man,
the man
who
Decided
to place the identity
of the people
on his sleeves
divine energy
shifting to songs
from generations.

The
flag
waves
as our hearts
dance along.

It houses.

our souls,

when

death

becomes physical,

a frequent,

visitor in our lives,
we lived on for a better tomorrow.

The forgotten

sons' and daughters' lives lost in time,

we're not in vain.

Here,

I knew my experience

was greater than mine. We are just pasting time, and I never

get
sensitive about much.

Though this reoccurs,

thought,

rampantly.

Wine takes time,

and we forget
a dream takes time
in
we cannot harness time.

As a man or woman,

we have forgotten,

how to be vulnerable.

It is not about wins,
losers or gains,

showing up and being seen, and committing to winning,
so, you build courage.

A

Talent Colonel,

John Garang de Mabior,

acknowledged,

you really cannot drive in the cheap seats of

your vision,

otherwise you will be taken on a joyride of

losses,

rather than playing in the arena.

A

Talent Colonel,

John Garang de Mabior,

acknowledged,

you really cannot drive in the cheap seats of

your vision,

otherwise you will be taken on a joyride of

losses,

rather than playing in the arena.

When
you armor up

for what is true,

and you direct your truth,
you welcome
your power through vulnerability,

a birthplace
of love and a dream.
I once chose,

forgiveness and never looked back.

I am not a politician.

I come with no policies,

to connect

with a common,
I have orphaned defeat.

I only have critics,

although

I am a part of a revelation,

who has

shown up
to the final dance.
A letter,
to the child, man or woman of South Sudan, note to self that our soil has become flooded with tears and anointed with our blood.
We have returned
within
belonging to an identity
as we belong
everywhere,

according to the liberation we proclaim.

SYNOPSIS

From Journal of a Refugee and Divinity Bior Aguer completes his memoir of poems with Revelation. A self-exploration of lived experiences and human will to live their truth. Bior Aguer takes readers on a journey to discovering themselves and gives us an insight into his mind.

Revelation
BIOR AGUER